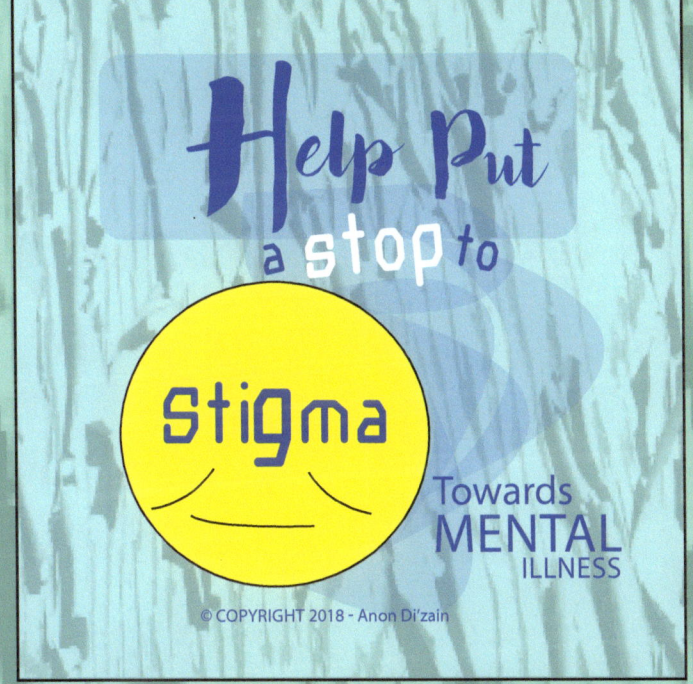

Help Put a stop to **Stigma** Towards MENTAL ILLNESS

© COPYRIGHT 2018 - Anon Di'zain

Written & Illustrated
By ANON DI'ZAIN

MELODIE RONE
BRENT CALHOUN

www.calwelldesign.com
www.anondizain.com
ISBN: 978-1537555249

This book was designed not only to inform, but also to get people, especially young people, to recognize and understand others as individuals as well as in relation to oneself.

S tigma lived alone in a common little house, on a ordinary street in an every day kind of town. Stigma didn't need anybody in his life as he believed he already knew what everyone was like. Due to this, Stigma lacked the color and excitement that all other color wheels have.

One day while returning from his run of the mill job, Stigma observed another color wheel picking flowers, looking so happy and content, when he heard a voice asking, "Would you like to have some flowers?". Stigma felt moved by seeing how happy this color wheel was, and decided to stop and talk for a few minutes.

stigma

Stigma found out her name was Complementary Colors. Complementary shared her story of picking wild flowers with her mother; Since the death of her mother, she had been dealing with depression. Up until today, Complementary didn't have anyone who noticed her picking flowers . The Depression surprised Stigma, as Complementary had looked so content and happy. Stigma believed he already knew that depressed people can't be happy.

Stigma said "Goodbye" to Complementary and went on his way, but couldn't help taking a little bit of her color with him. He didn't know what it meant, but it was something to think about.

Stigma, feeling different after his meeting, had decided that what he felt was nothing more than hunger. Stigma decided he would go to the ordinary bakery to get something to eat. When Stigma got to the bakery he noticed that it had changed, with new lighting, a colorful background, and what seemed to be a happy but quite anxious baker. Although the baker's behavior seemed out of the ordinary Stigma's hunger made him enter the bakery for his usual cupcake.

Stigma went to order his usual cupcake from the baker named Modified Triad, but upon ordering, Stigma was asked how he would like his cupcake. Stigma had always had the usual ordinary cupcake, but to his surprise found there were many variations of cupcakes. There was a variety of shapes, flavors, added this, without that, and yet not one single ordinary cupcake.

Stigma didn't know what to do, there was three of everything. Modified Triad seemed to notice that Stigma was having difficulties, and asked if he could help. Stigma asked "Why are there so many cupcakes?" Modified Triads' answer surprised Stigma even more than all the cupcakes. Modified Triad told Stigma that he felt that there should be a cupcake perfectly suited for every person. He went on to tell Stigma that due to a disorder called Obsessive Compulsion Disorder he will not stop until each cupcake is perfect.

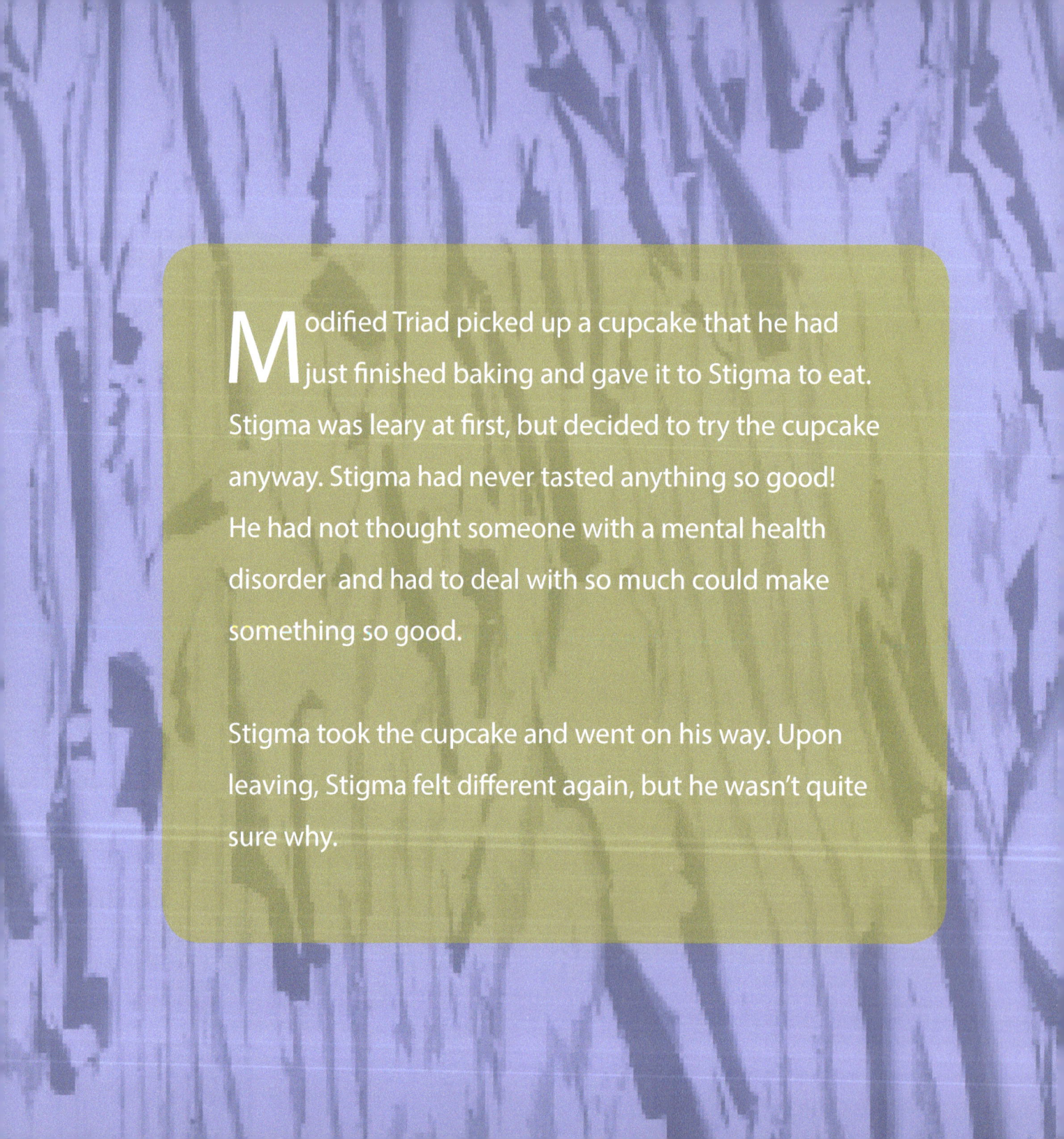

Modified Triad picked up a cupcake that he had just finished baking and gave it to Stigma to eat. Stigma was leary at first, but decided to try the cupcake anyway. Stigma had never tasted anything so good! He had not thought someone with a mental health disorder and had to deal with so much could make something so good.

Stigma took the cupcake and went on his way. Upon leaving, Stigma felt different again, but he wasn't quite sure why.

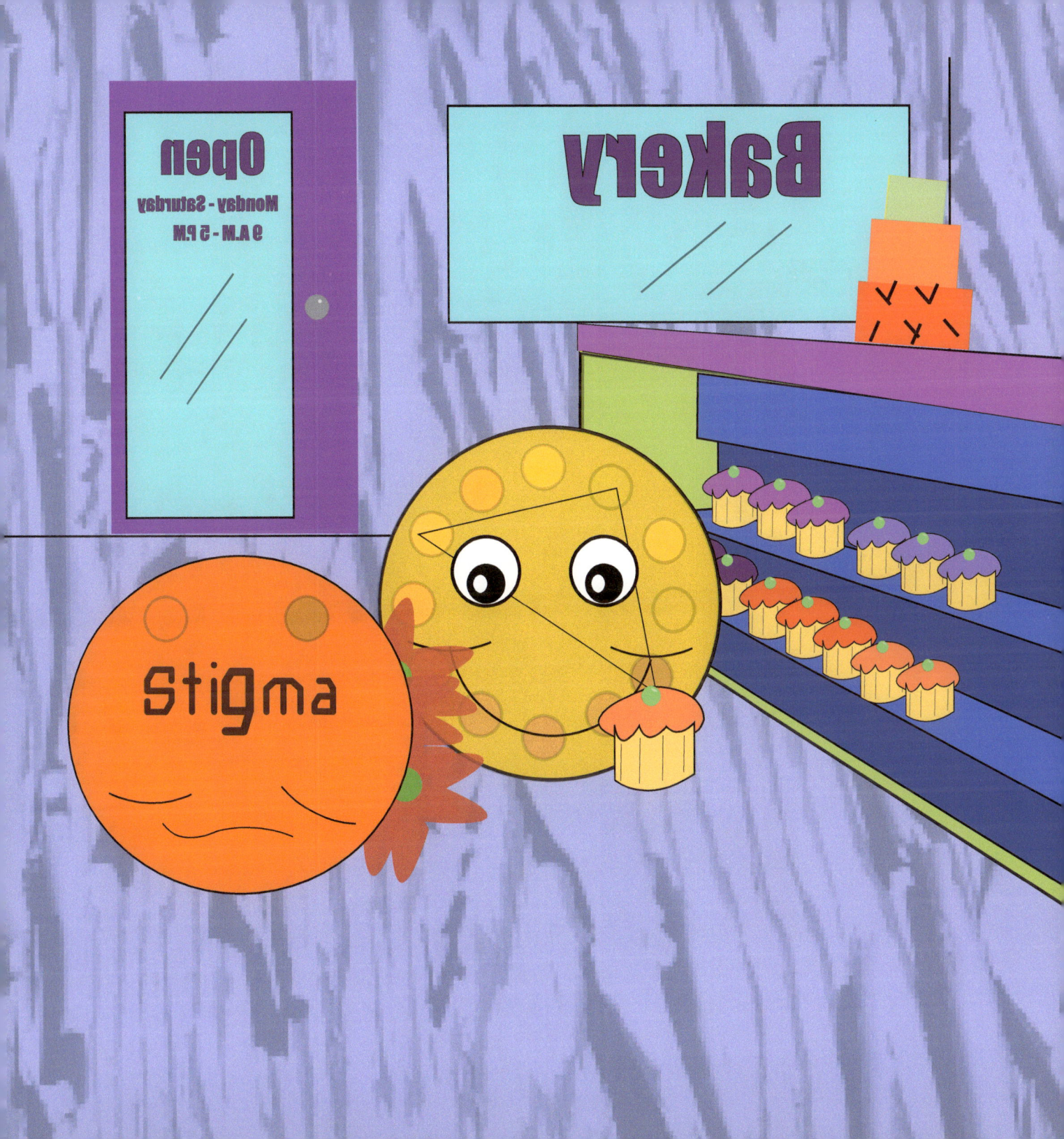

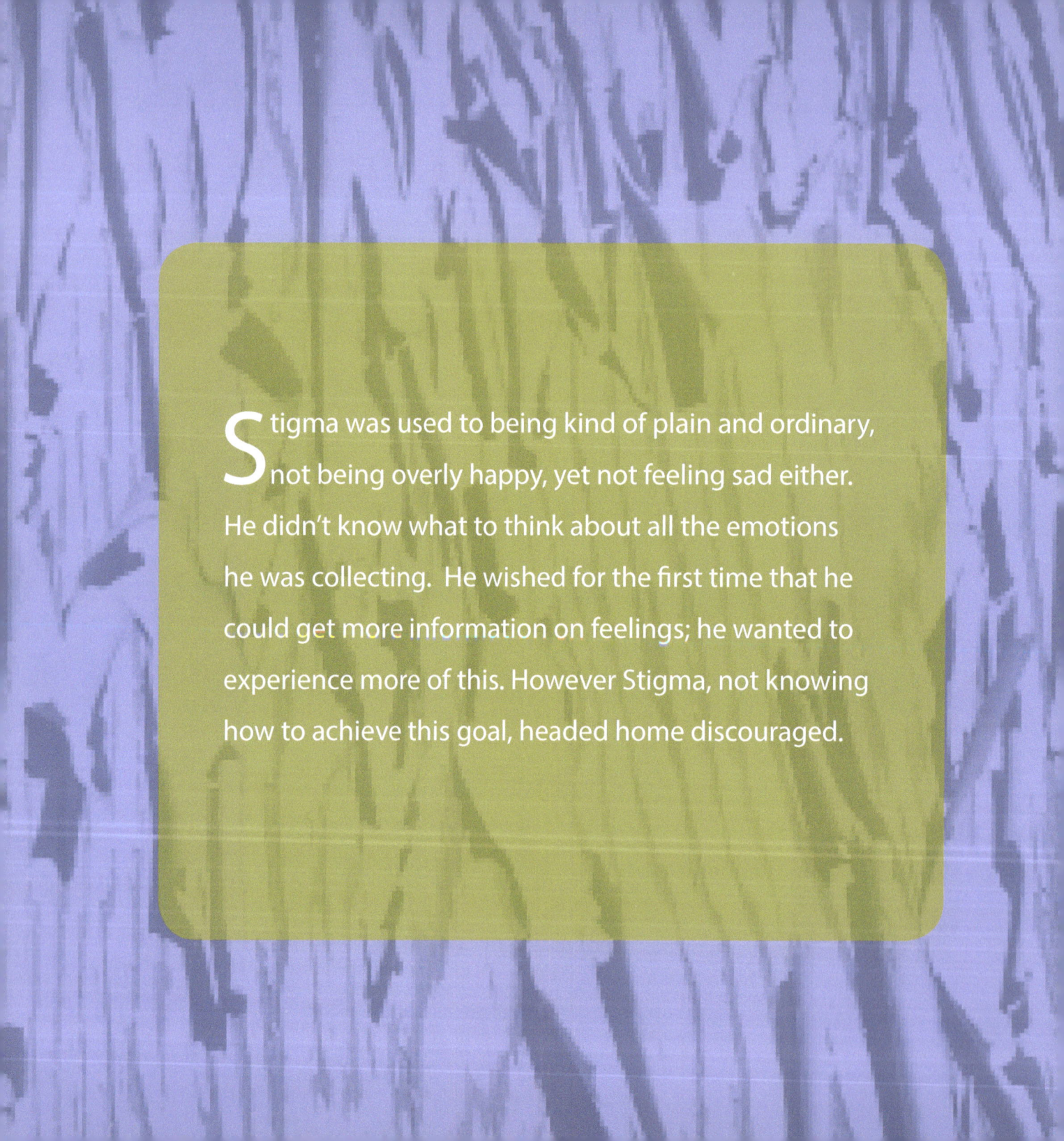

Stigma was used to being kind of plain and ordinary, not being overly happy, yet not feeling sad either. He didn't know what to think about all the emotions he was collecting. He wished for the first time that he could get more information on feelings; he wanted to experience more of this. However Stigma, not knowing how to achieve this goal, headed home discouraged.

Back on his way home he saw what appeared to be the most colorful wheel yet. Although upon reaching her, he realized that for a color wheel she seemed very sad. Stigma didn't understand this. Why was the color wheel so full of color yet so gloomy? Stigma who didn't want to go back to being plain and ordinary, approached this unusual color wheel. Even though she was crying, she was still able to smile and say "Hello".

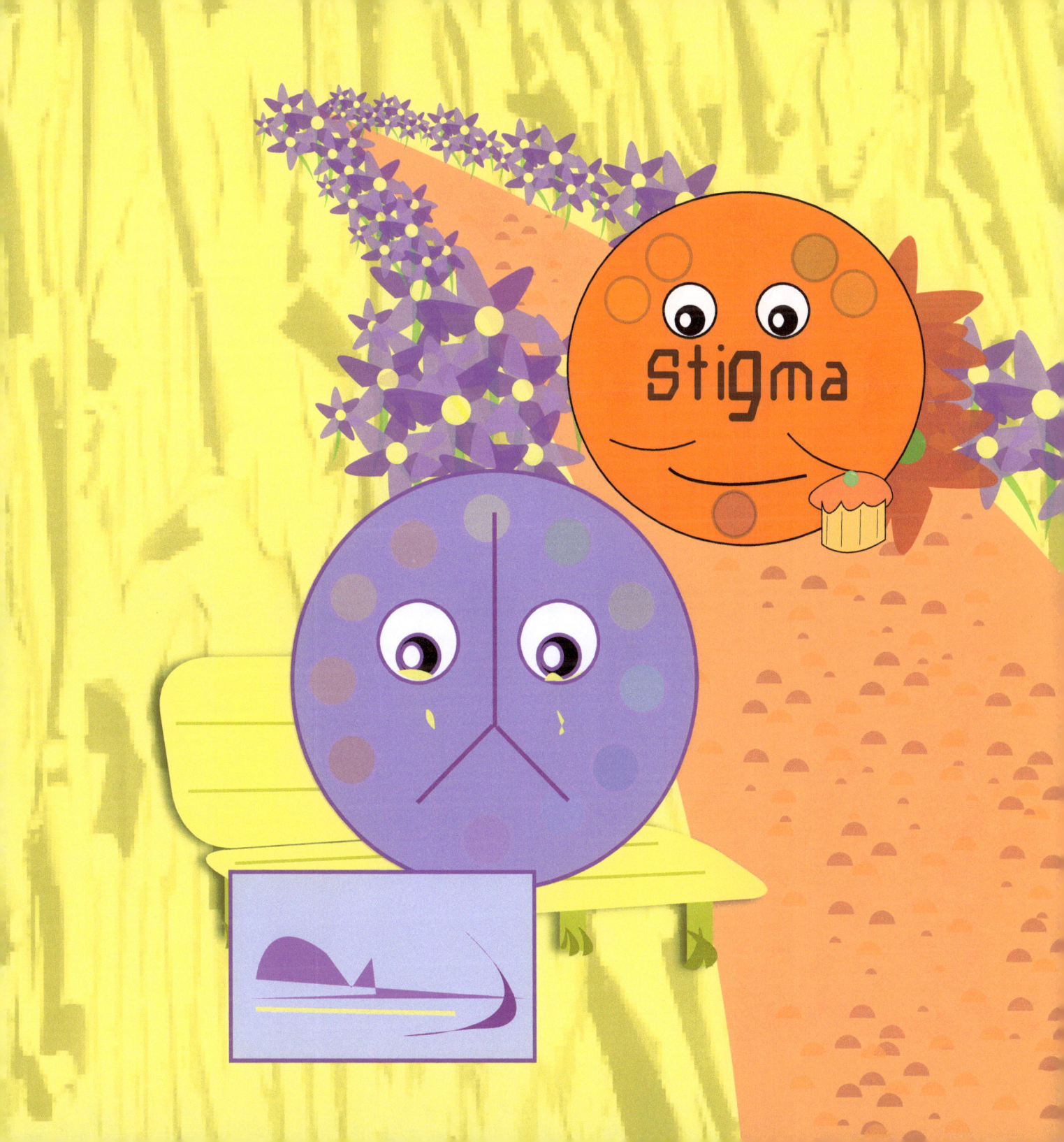

She looked up at Stigma and introduced herself as Split Complementary. Stigma, seeing that she was sad, asked, "What has made you feel so disappointed?" Split Complementary held up a painting that she was holding and explained that she had wanted to create something extraordinary in class, only to have a few of the students criticize her accomplishment.

Stigma looked at the painting and told Split Complementary that he thought it was a very fine painting, well beyond his ability. Stigma noticed that the more he complimented her on the painting, the more she seemed to cheer up. This made Stigma feel good. He had never sat and talked to someone, or helped someone. Stigma noticed that Split Complementary seemed a very caring person, but she looked down on herself, and after the criticism of others, didn't have the faith to believe her efforts were wonderful. Stigma told Split Complementary, that her art should be made for enjoyment without regard to what anyone else thinks about it....That's why it's called art.

Split Complementary asked Stigma to keep the painting in return for all the help he had given her. Stigma had never had anyone give him anything so special. This made him feel warm inside: yet another emotion he had never experienced before.

Stigma found out how he had been misjudging others. Stigma now feels he can achieve anything. Stigma, who didn't want to go back to his ordinary life, decided to change his name to Analogous. Now that he is full of color, Analogous plans to use his own colors to help others.

CHANGE stigma Towards MENTAL ILLNESS

By Getting Informed

SPACE RESERVED
FOR CONTACT
INFORMATION